YEAR OF THE FIRES

YEAR OF THE FIRES

AND OTHER POEMS

by Joyce Nower

A publication of the Center for Women's Studies and Services
San Diego

Copyright © 1983 by Joyce Nower

Library of Congress Catalog Number: 81-70725
ISBN 0 - 9600856-2-9 (paper)

Printed in the United States of America
First Edition

Graphic by Lenore Simon

Published and distributed by the Center for Women's Studies
and Services (CWSS), *Year of the Fires*, 908 "E" Street, San
Diego, CA 92101.

FOR LEON . . . .

who knows that survival is food, clothing, shelter, and art

ACKNOWLEDGMENTS

The author and the publisher gratefully acknowledge
the following magazines, newspapers, and anthologies
in which some of the poems in this book originally
appeared: *The Greater Golden Hill Poetry Express,
The Longest Revolution, Rainbow Snake, C/O, Good
Times, Womansoul, Anthology of California Women
Poets, New Voices, Lemming Review, Cafe Solo,
Deepest Valley Review, The Laughing Unicorn, North
American Mentor Magazine, Mosaic,* and *New Voices.*

The author also wishes to acknowledge composer Joyce
Lane for setting the following poems to music: I Move
Toward Stillness, Fiesta de la Virgen, Colette at Age
Five: In Her Style, Poems to Night I and II, and Age
Thirteen.

FOREWORD

In *Journey Around My Room*, Louise Bogan holds that the quality we know as "talent" nurtures the writer's power. No doubt a ho-hum observation unless we take that definition further as did the ancients. Talent, in the classical sense, is a gift of the Muses, the Daughters of Memory.

Skipping a few eons and cultures, the idea of talent is revived in what the French call *le souffle de génie*—"the breath of inspiration." No doubt, Joyce Nower owns the gift and has been visited, in one guise or another, by a daughter of memory, a giver of breath and breadth.

What is mirrored in her poems is a breadth and generosity of spirit that is clear, active and knowable. And how refreshing it is, after reading the collection, to be in touch with a woman wrestling with themes including but not limited by uterine concerns.

Also in evidence is a musical ear delicately tuned to the melodies of a sensual earth. Seldom does Nower stray from Ezra Pound's dictum: "poetry begins to atrophy when it gets too far from music." Listen to the assonance and alliteration in "Poem to Night II":

> The night bird sings
> and I sing back at him.
> From olive to pepper
> to oak to thorn he
> carries the sacred
> alphabet of balm
> pried from the bark
> by a hungry beak. . .

And that is only one instance. Color and tone resonate throughout the collection, saying something about the poet's painterly eye. Seduced by the visual world, by its offerings and largesse, she names and inventories with a poet's benediction.

The illusion that Nower is hooked largely into the abundance
of things is sometimes shattered. Here the journey turns inward:

> . . . my big brown hands resting
> in my lap, my swimmer's legs etched beneath
> the soft blue folds of my dress, my big
> red walking shoes planted firmly on the floor . . .

What shines through the poems is a portrait of a gutsy woman
who can write of "looking forward to her destination," secure in
"the right to outstare time and the works of men." Even as Nower
pauses to ruminate on trees, flowers and birds, these are only rest
stops in a larger voyage that weaves beyond the circle of home.

At a time of widespread anomie and blurred connections,
Nower's passion about social issues is as admirable as it is uncom-
mon. "Requiem in Memory of a South American Revolutionary,"
whose incantatory richness is mindful of Garcia Lorca, highlights
a collection in which intimacies and dramatic counterpoints share
at least one thing: a positive attitude unmarred, as is so much work
today, by pretentiousness and solemnity.

Nower's outbound journey has its fitting climax in the longest
poem within a well-organized collection. "Voices in the Blood" is
a heady challenge to the kind of flippancy creeping today into
poetry-as-reportage: the trivializing of serious events, the shrinking
of them into minimal forms. It speaks of Nazi outrage, the abiding
love for a survivor, and it does so with seemliness and restraint. With
fullness, and securely under the command of a poet whose affirm-
ing warmth asserts itself, the voyage goes on.

> . . . And so we have come to twenty years of love —
> beyond song, dark eyes, love-making in murphy
> beds, against fence posts, behind the stern
> stone lions in the city . . . park;
> having run a course between the dull gulp
> of domesticity and the ceaseless terminations
> of this neurotic time . . .

Here in closing is a typical illumination of what is keenly felt in a
collection of poetry that matters.

Colette Inez

CONTENTS

I. Birth

Birth

The child at the window
sees the bay stretched taut,
then wrinkle as clouds
eclipse the sun. The
sky turns white and drifts.
She feels herself mount
through the glass, sees her
human shape, now touched
by air and bay, grow
strange and vast; watches it
flicker a zigzag
brightness in the sky;
sees it turn and face
her, and in the sharpest
gust of wind descend
back through the glass;
feels it slide against
her inner skin, spread
from stomach to legs, from
chest to head, feels
it grasp her brain, and
kiss it. She looks at
her hands, inspects the
soft hairs curved slightly,
and sees the skin grow
taut beneath her eyes.

Poem to Night I

Black night and trees and moon and bird all sing
to me. I move beyond the pall of light
into the dark and watch myself dissolve
in dark, turn to shadows that hide the tips
of olive twigs, the silver veins of snails,
the coarse gold field grass. I am at home.
I was at home when as a child in bed
I'd watch the ancient moon stare back at me,
hear hoofbeats hit the air, a cry descend
the trees, and feeling handled with desire
would glide from moonlight deep inside myself
and getting up would dance in naked joy
outside the ring of light upon the floor
to celebrate the silence of the world.

Age Thirteen

She wades into the shallows
her body arched back in praise of her breasts
her arms outstretched
on the brightness of the East and West.

Beside the nets of summer fishermen she kneels
and feels the knock of flesh against her hands
and rising laughing shakes loose the fragrance
of seaweed, sea, and sand.

The Glass Candy Dish

The glass candy dish
I bought for you
at the church bazaar
and broke on the stairs
before you saw it —
for thirty years, Mother,
I have searched it out
in gift stores
and junk shops:

a cut glass goblet
with flowers etched on it
aloft a slender stem
with a tiny perked cap
rising to a perfect ball
for finger and thumb to lift.

I did not imagine it
heavy with chocolate bits
the shadow passing
through the delicate blooms,
a loam
to bury sorrow in;
or holding jelly beans—
reds, yellows, greens—
a maypole of tastes
luminous honied eggs
multi-colored bulbs
glowing
beckoning
all sweet tooths
forward;

but by itself
empty clear pure
ah what it would have
looked like
on the polished cherrywood buffet
o lustrous prism
its image doubled
in the beveled mirror—
something of beauty:
what a snowflake
would be like
under father's glass,
or a teardrop
suspended
holding light.

I brought instead
a substitute
a smooth ceramic vase
mustard-colored squat —
o toad of objects
beast slouching near the rose
rude gnome among the guests —
and you thanked me
and placed a spray
of flowers in it.

I glimpsed
the dish again, Mother,
or so I thought,
only recently,
in a gift shop clutter

but looking closer
saw a crude double
a pink glass cup
with a gold frill
a cap with ridges
and a gold leaf handle —
the fluttering, not the steady eye —
but not before
I had quivered and sighed
and felt again that grief
that as a child had made me cry
but had gone unspoken
that in my hands
such beauty
had been broken.

Poem to Night II

The nightbird sings
and I sing back at him.
From olive to pepper
to oak to thorn he
carries the sacred
alphabet of balm
pried from the bark
by a hungry beak.
Deceptive priest,
giver and taker of shadows,
are you the spirit
of my father
come for forgiveness
or to forgive?
I cry out the
human cry that
never changes
and try to catch
his meaning to
reply, but in my mind
the singing always dies.

Comfort

When you sleep beside me
and the dream breaks through
like a knife through flesh

and you see grandfather
told to clear the way
spit on the boot
and leather fingers shoot
him down in the street

and you hear mother
hand over hand
feeling fingers that played
nocturnes grow numb
cry out a solo terror

while the town — cottage
and manor, row upon row
of chestnut and silver birch —
dies out like a coal
in a crater of snow

and you see your ways defiled —
a people's song in blood
spilt on scorched ground,
and you, nameless, exiled
from those legendary plains:

I turn to you then
when the knife of the dream cuts bone
and you moan from that deep;

I cradle your head in my arms
and comfort myself back to sleep.

Gardening

Everything grows lush within your sight:
You look at me — my breasts rise up a nipple's
    height.

Colette at Age 5: In Her Style

She strides into her mind.
Emerging queen,
she decrees
the capture of the seas.

That done, she boards the ship,
inspects the sails,
the fighting force,
then deftly sets the course.

How graceful on the bridge
in silver robes,
a wand of gold.
A wave — and stars unfold.

She signals to her fish;
commands the gull
on the lee
to keep her company.

And now she storms the fort
which crests the moon.
In the arch
unwary soldiers march.

This is her empire now:
the coursing seas,
vagrant skies
are bounded by her eyes.

Two Sides of Broccoli

You state vehemently
that you will never eat broccoli:
it tickles going down;
it tastes like weeds, or as ground
fresh-plowed in the spring must taste.
And yet here you stand
with a half-formed head in your hand
severed from our vegetable garden,
a head covered with winsom
yellow broccoli flowers,
and isn't it lovely.

Imagine, acre on acre
of blossoming plant. Pleased
I give thanks, and
put it into a vase, and
place it on the kitchen table,
from all sides visible.
A few days pass
and a swinish gas
floats up from the thing.
I see the kitchen fill up with
field upon flowering field
of the ripening nosegay
growing up Salinas way.

My nose is full again
of the odor rising from the floor
of the green valley,
even though the car did sixty,
and I remember thinking
of cow dung and potatoes rotting,
of pond water left in a capped jar,
and body smells in a closed car.

Son, on second thought,
but from another angle,
I can really see your point.

October Morning

It is a morning still and sweet as this —
light mellow on the broad poinsettia leaves,
the clean air swept by the languid pepper tree,
daisies, some browning, some in bloom —

Have you noticed that mint grows near old faucets
my son observes as we stand arm in arm on the lawn,
the part-Siamese cat stretched out in sunlight,
the silence twanging like a plucked string

across the day, across a darkened era
of poisoned jungles where the amber sparrowhawk
once stalked the sky, and the big cat cries
mouth muffled in her fur; of women —

rabbits — dressed up in scars, sacred
signs exiled in a brutal memory;
across nations born from loss of profit
and continents controlled by the cyclop's eye.

On and on the dreary list of human fates
nailed up in a market place staked out by captains
but where they seldom ride. No ethic now seems
sound but force: the whip incites the peasant's knife.

It is on just such a morning as this,
when October light hallows our heads
and deep quiet hymns up from the hedge
and I breathe in this aspect of nature

that I touch once again my own roots —
the moon my sister, the sun a kindly friend,
the elements and animals their go-betweens,
predator turned innocent again —

that I restore myself to a way,
to a poise of season and leaf,
that allows me to sleep in the night
that moves my heart through the day.

II. Year of the Fires

Year of the Fires

The fury of it unexpected
and the spiteful wind
behind the wheel of fire

drove it mercilessly
day and night
around the simmering city.

The southern hills cracked open
and the scorched plain
stretched and split.

One by one we died,
were maimed, or turned
strange in our charred hearts.

I searched you out, love,
between the shocking birth
and rumor bitter as ruins

when each in her own search
cut with a scavenger beak
the circuit of another's life.

But you were nowhere
to be found, love, out fighting fire
with fire in another part of town.

Only myself, an instinct to preserve,
a survivor, running
from the dangling wires.

A broken heart is like that —
a disconnection from a center —
and its repair —

O blind faith in shoots on the scarred oak,
in the tawny rabbit,
even the hawk's eye —

A deep waiting in the quiet lair,
the laborious gestation,
at last the rising heart breaking into air.

Report from the Desert

FOR L. C.

Over the clean white page
a hand holds the pen
that charts my case:
the hand — age forty — lined
like the layered limestone we saw
in the cliffs near Flagstaff
or like a pueblo structure
brick staggered on thin brick,
a culture rising from a lava mesa,
vaulted up out of its own rock,
baked in the centuries' sun,
indigenous, ancestral,
proud, quick to feel,
honorable, dangerous, destroyed.

We here have been aged
in the sun beyond our time.
Earthbrown, burnt red,
our two feet lope
with ancient purpose,
caught on a new path
closer to the ridge;
our fingers, tufted
with vestigial hairs,
haul the burden of ourselves
up an asphalt hill;
our hearts — my dear heart! —
that once had
familiar purpose, die
in crosscurrents that wash
away the mind, until all
is steel shaft and wire.

Then what survives within?
What cunning absolute
inches steadily forward
beneath the crass exchanges
of power, the protestations?
Survival, and aboriginal will:
the ultimate desire
of the scorned, the betrayed,
the loved and the unloved
to live out a life,
to put together
the fragments of a self.

No culture remains forever —
values glorious vainglorious die.
Few human ties survive,
and madness moves behind the change.
Beloved people and beloved objects
are betrayed, reassembled,
and betrayed again.
Dear friend, consciousness sears
but cannot go out.

See here, as simple proof,
my two bare arms,
my hand, these strange words
in our common mother tongue,
survivors in a world
that has come apart.
Conveyors of will,
but with the mark of dread,
they move together on down this page
across this empty space.

Fillet

These four small fish
my son pulled in
lie side by side
in the white enamel sink.

Brought up under a wet sky,
out of a lake flickering
with black and white lights,
they were caught without pleasure.

No prayer went up or down
to the heaven of fish. The
observatory tower on the lake's
edge remained empty.

According to custom
it is my turn now
to finish out the ritual
with a sharp knife.

One by one
I saw the four heads off,
slit four bellies,
scoop out four tiny guts,
and chop off fins and tails.

Eight miniature fillets —
barely a few mouthfuls,
not worth the sullen day.
And such blind surgery!

I dreamt of a woman once
of character and pride
her aura scales of gold
glowing from her shores,

who unprepared
at finding herself
gasping
on the cutting block

proceeded to cut off
her own head, her dumb mouth
not able to utter,
the tongue thickening in blood;

the brain reduced to the run
of the knife;
sliced off her fins,
becoming quieter and quieter;

scraped, until the once shining scales
that had marked her way
were piled neatly, a memory,
at her side.

After Silence

FOR S. K.

I.

Willing once brought back the dead;
brought back Lazarus, his hands and feet stiff
in his dead clothes, a tatter on his face.

Called out, the stone removed, he walked
on faith, that miraculous rag, after flapping
four days in the dark, sensing,

but not quite, the cold, touching
but not quite, his own moldering breast;
reborn in broad daylight, with his sisters,

some neighbors, and their returned friend watching,
comparing, each in her own mind,
his walk, his turn of thought, his grey skin

with her own. Enviable him, brought back by the strain,
the pressure, the sweat of their longing to heal,
to return his life to the earth.

Watching me — my look, my talk, my silence —
you would perform a miracle, but times change,
and death comes now in numerous ways.

Sometimes it's a matter of slow amputations —
the heart here, the mouth there, finally
the dendrites sliced to staunch the pain.

See me, for example, boiled down to a senseless
essence, a dried apple peel,
an outline.

Recite the list again: a birth, fires melting
streets and sounds, encroachments against
the familiar, signs of invisible changes

flashing on and off like neons,
and the absences of love like a body
bloated dragged from the water drowned —

all these temporal matters shot to a heart
that knows the tone and texture
of the Void and goes easily on from there.

II.

Rather the complication lies in dealing
with Everything: feeling the force of It
moving down through time,

the harmony and rightness
of the wheel of Woman
of the wheel of Man

alike and different
bright diamond disks
that churn the air

with an apartness
and with an interaction,
arms and legs locking,

breast on breast, arm on leg,
hand on back with joyful
familiarity,

the awesome freedom of the human
sexes apart and together
man with man

woman with man
with child both
woman with woman

naked complements
the love wheel glistening
and the air humming.

III.

But in the bathroom once
crouched next to the sink
(my eyes grown older in the glass!)

It came looking for me.
Out of the swirling luster
that wheeled from the ceiling

fierce eyes stared at me!
at me! knocked the wind from me!
nailed me to the floor!

and then the earthen face
emerged, neither male nor female,
the piercing face of the Sage,

the Force, the Destiny, that Thing
inside, outside —
destroyer, preserver, creator —
I clutched myself and wailed.

IV.

All this and more has dulled me now.
The red yarn love-ball that once hung
in the window has been misplaced.

I have become a sexless thing
waiting for rebirth into another aeon.
O sisters, hear me now

in my bone-cold cell
trying to escape the suicidal gap
between the dream and me,

trying to reweave the broken threads.
I drift!   I drift!
It is survival now,

the bared teeth, the craft, the brute
strength to move the boulder
from the mouth!

Act III

Up here on the second floor
under steep eaves
in what was once an attic
I sit upright in bed.

I am on stage,
the nightlight my spotlight.
One bed. One bureau. One planter.
One high-backed chair.

Faces crowd the uncurtained windows,
and in the shadows
ranged in neat rows,
others wait to see Act III.

I wind the clock and yawn.
"How naturally
she performs,
as if she were at home!"

When I reach out to turn the radio off,
a voice whispers:
"How clever
to end the play at bedtime!"

Pretending to arrange the sheets
I glance quickly at the briefcase
on the chair.
It holds the secret.

Without *it*, they will approximate my motives,
only half guess
with what feelings
I do the things I do.

They will have to settle on the feelings
they would have.
After all,
what is drama for?

Of course, they will
discuss me, regardless.
That is, to be sure,
their part.

But should it somehow fall into their hands,
I will not
go on tomorrow.
I'll cancel the show.

I can hear them shifting in their seats,
clearing their throats,
breathing harder
towards the stage.

Used to managing my own show,
I shut off the light,
turn my back on them,
and settle down to sleep.

Aesthetic of Sanity

I. FROM THE WIDOW'S WALK

Wings folded, throbbing, in my heart
the great bird cannot sing
for fear, not of the wet sea air
methodically whipping the slender palms,
nor of the beach lip dissolving in foam,
or of the dark figure on the motorbike,
the skyscrapers pursuing like spikes,
but that the wind and the palms,
the buildings, that dark figure, and the sea,
at any moment, pulled askew
by the magnet of the mind
into other shades and shapes,
may expose some close intangible crime.

II. DAWN

The sun rises now.
Soon the avocado will glisten,
the window glass in the house
next door will reflect the sun,
the tinsel bay will mask
the occasional ship,
and the curving freeway
maintain the staged brightness
of its moving colors.
It must all come and go,
move back and forth in the eyeball
without a hitch,
with a hard decisiveness
like a bright brass rail.
For if one line should run,
one color drip onto another,
the overfull mind
like a brush heavy with paint
will banish what lies before it
with a swift malignant stroke.

The Vision

FOR L. N.

At the moment, Krishna, when violet moons rose above the bed
   on which we lay, our brown limbs close and beautiful,
      love an oil on our skin,

I saw against the body's glow the passage of the human herd
   over an indifferent earth: I saw men and women bending
      in dense fields, harvesting their single row of wheat,

sometimes in sorrow, sometimes in joy, while in the woods nearby
   indifferent eyes taxed the human gain; beyond the woods,
      I saw mounted riders deploying spies to the forest's edge;

and dimly from the far off ocean rocks I heard prophetic words
   all lost in wind and sand to all but one soul doomed to understand;
      and up from gray-coiffed cities came mutterings

of bewilderment, and I strained to see, and saw above one gray town
   a great stone mother crying tears down into the ruined streets
      where only women walked; and here and there, across

the vastness, the martyrs of the species emerged in fixed positions:
   dismembered limbs on altars (Hail Hypatia! Witch of Alexandria!), or
      crouched in jails, their beliefs banished, or wandering in exile.

And then nothing, nothing there, and across that nothing
   piping merrily the Skiffle Band, sweet and tender
      in their passing, knowing how to walk on air;

And I, exultant, purged of fear, outrageously merry with the truth
   and arbitrary courage of that fluting into air,
      looked on in godlike ease and watched the changes:

this time more symbols of the human journey rose: the firegiver,
   the seeker among the dead, the fallen angel, the winged boy,
      the enlightened one, the warrior maid, the crucified son —

at that moment I longed for the life of my own son, and saw
    the dark bitterness of his going and felt a wild lusting
        for the destruction of the hunters — a crouching

of muscle, a heat in the head, to kill with pleasure with bare hands
    or like a lion to spring to kill clean to protect her cubs —
        and I feared what I felt;

then your face, Krishna, brown and lively beneath black matted hair,
    collapsed into the swirling lines of the Destroyer
        and I began to know two aspects of your nature:

I felt the weight of that rage that you in some other life had
    grappled with when alone in the snow of war your beloved friend
        had died in the helpless circle of your homeless arms

and I felt beyond that, companion, to the deep compassion, not nearly
    mine, and the crush of the struggle to it, and the looming
        aloneness of it,

                    o strange spirit
                come down through time
                    to be with me
            in this time and this place
                with this burden of flesh
            and the terror and the weight
                        of it
                burning out a holy place
                        within
            and I knew you then at that moment
                as no one had before
            and I glimpsed the depth of my own future
                    movement
                and with terror
        the passage toward my own re-incarnation.

I Move Toward Stillness

I move toward stillness
as if in a current
standing,
sensing the moving waters,
the bobbing eyes,
and the soundless blue claw
scuttling.

Movement rings
my stillness, rings
it roughly, like water
ringing rock.
It is the rock I love.
With hermit hardness.
Withstanding.

But it is of the current too —
shaped by it,
shaping.
So I am —
there's no escaping —
shaped by it,
shaping.

III. Requiem

Sloan Canyon Songs

FOR M. S.

I. THE ARRIVAL

Dawn, and the crouching sun breaks over the hill
to flash a signal to the chaparral

and to the uncoiling vertebrae of rock;
I glow as I hit the crest, then suddenly drop

from chest to feet
into a brushwood sea where manzanita

waves a warning at my gun, at the hostile
nimbus of the steel barrel.

II. THE HUNTER

The sparrow hawk
marks off an arc
then props herself
against a shelf
of air. Hawk
eyes stalk me.
As I aim
I sense the fling
of spotted wings.

III. THE MINE

At midday we reach a mine
dug by some old rough
who plodded months at a time
for gold; Milton stuffs
dry brush into a branch hollow,
lights it, and leads us on.
One by one we follow
into the catacomb:
a processional of eyes
and fingers touch the vein
that bleeds along the wall
and down into the groin
of earth, where, as legend
has it, the miner, his veins
turned gold, remained.
Earth lays the final claim.

Tijuana Graveyard

The poor lie
beneath these simple stones
the local priest had painted
some in aqua, some in pink.

He stood a sandstone angel
at the splintering gate,
its wings half-folded,
one already chipped.

I drive by again
and look:
the fluted wings drift
backwards toward the dead.

Beyond the grave
down where the living are
strung out in two small lines
of huts along the road, he stares

day after day, his hands
cast into prayer
that can do nothing to wipe
away the stains that yellow

the countryside, for where
pupils should be are
blank corneas of stone.

Fiesta de la Virgen

Among young men the Virgin moves
brown breasts and shoulders molded with gold foil;
on her throat bright beads lie.

Slender fingers pinch her torso
·sweet with the smell of rubbed jasmine
gently
and silk shirts graze her breasts.

On an altar spread with starched white linen
they place her with her painted eyes
glancing out on curtseying pink flounces,
belts and boots and dancing thighs,
male eyes.

Night falls. In the darkened skies
the fireworks come suddenly
like quivering rods of heat.
The worshipers stir; children cry

as if a hand had jerked the beads from off that neck
and scattered gold foil
with a sigh.

The Beginning

We turn our heads away in fear
for it has come to us at last

just as the gold gleams most brightly
and the engines move moonward

to write in code upon the wall
the dangerous turning in our hearts,

for we see blood at the column base,
have discerned in the bending shadows

behind the master on his horse
the bending shadow of the slave

and in alleyways have had to face
our brothers fighting for the scraps

while somewhere high in granite buildings
accustomed eyes arrange matters

about us, here in the shadow, too,
waiting, our words at last decoded,

feeling the flower of treason unfold
delicately in the sun of our hearts.

Lament

When the moon goes out
and the heroes have
ripped off their masks
so we can see the single
face beneath —
Some whom I have known will die.

When the gloved hand holding flowers moves
closer to the cape
and steel glints
among the buds —
Some whom I have known will die.

Some whose lips I kissed —
that man, his wife,
the girl whose face I stroked —
by the rope, a knife —
whose hair I ruffled
in the dead of night —
by a shot, fire —
one whom I desire,
whose body spoke to me
before his lips —
by the lash, the whip,
the two-edged blade —
whose hand I laid on mine
whose body I perfumed —
by the stone, the cross —
whose moral being impassioned
me to love —
by the ship, the tank,
the plane, the club.

When the moon goes out
and the deathwatch starts
to tick away our lives —
fierce with love and pride
we'll put the deathmask
on our varied faces,
line up, and stand alert.

Requiem in Memory of a South American Revolutionary

For Leon

Mezzo Soprano (the Nun)
Alto (the Mother)
Tenor (First Friend)
Bass (Second Friend)

I. REQUIEM (The Nun)

It was done. It is done.
It will be done again.
As long as some own land
and some the arms that plow
hearts will long for the land
on which they labor and they
will name that longing freedom;
and justice will be fields of ripening wheat.

Will the violence never cease?
Will we ever move past this?
Let flesh help flesh resist
until the world's dark blood
sings out one common song
in praise of land and grain.
Let its refrain be peace,
and peace again, and again.

"Requiem aeternam dona eis"
"Grant them eternal rest"

II. KYRIE (First Friend)

She was not there.   *"Kyrie eleison"*
She did not know   *"Lord, have mercy upon us"*
the crime took place.
We told her later
face to face
how the State dealt with him
called traitor;
how they nailed her son
to the bare plank wall,
cut off his feet,
a runner's feet;
how they crucified him
as a lesson
by the State.

III. QUID SUM MISER (The Mother)

Pain swells in me   *"Quid sum miser tunc dicturus?"*
like a foetus   *"What pain exceeds mine?"*
in a throbbing belly.
The fingers, toes, and vertebrae
of pain struggle to get out.
Too late.
In dreams each night
you come too late.

IV. LIBER SCRIPTUS (The Nun)

Police drove to his farm
where he lived alone
behind rubber trees and corn
on the western edge of town.
Arrived at dusk after
the garden had been watered
when the day's work done
he had laid out knives
on the stone, cut down
the cured goat hides
from the pole beneath the eaves
and set about to carve
the story of the town in stone.
They they had come.
Some one had informed,
said he carried contraband,
hid fugitives,
ran messages
for the revolution.

"Liber scriptus proferetur"
"Now the record shall be cited"

V. LACRYMOSA (First Friend)

We found him at sunup
nailed like a carved wood
jesus on the wall.
Sweat clouded our eyes, Mother.
We sweated our fear.
We could not hear
his heart,
could not hear
the dim breath stirring.
We strained our eyes
and did not believe his death.

"Lacrymosa dies illa"
"What weeping on that day"

VI. INGEMISCO (Second Friend)

We took a stick
and gently forced the nails out.
We did not let the body drop.
We removed it gently.
We removed the feet
hacked from the steely ankles
and laid him on the stone
my coat for a pillow.
We washed the limbs
that ran towards revolution.
The Sister dressed him
in the shirt with red birds
at the throat and the woven pants —
your last gift, Mother.
He is buried in the field
his tools wrapped in goatskin
beside him. Earthbound
the eagle, our hovering eye.
Who knows the way?
Who carries our cry?

"Ingemisco tanquam reus"
"Hear my weeping and my wailing"

VII. CONFUTATIS (The Mother)

The night his friends arrived here with the news
I saw him at the moment of his death.
I dreamed he held the killers with an eye,
then calmly sent his spirit from that place
as he told me he did — as in a game —
when running over hardened jungle paths
from secret place to secret place, his feet
and legs would start to bleed from twigs and stones;
and his dry throat bursting into flame,
he'd will the pounding of his feet and heart
to move him to a second, third, and fourth
wind until like the wind his pain soared on.

"Confutatis maledictis"

"While the wicked are confounded"

VIII. TUBA MIRUM (First Friend)

O shining legs of the runner —   *"Tuba mirum spargens sonum"*
tone, pride, anger
in limbs that dodged ruts,   *"A wondrous sound rings from*
wandering chickens,   *the trumpet"*
the beaded snake;
that fled
soundless in the soundless
density of leaves
from town to town,
carrying the armed message
to those who starve
for land and bread —
now dead!

IX. DIES IRAE (The Mother)

Stone melts in flame.   *"Dies irae, dies illa"*
Flames ring the soul   *"Day of anger, day of mourning"*
and a vast canyon dents the earth.
Will succumbs, and the struggle stops.
The once shining legs
lie broken on cold stone.
I watch them
and drift voluptuously on hate.
My moral being slips away.
My fist clenches my knife
and I enact the various deaths
by knife the torturers will suffer —
I see the places where my knife will enter.
The desire for destruction grows
as vast as the sky.
I drift in it.

X. FERTORIUM: DOMINE JESU CHRISTE
(The Nun)

Mind, turn carefully
on his fate.
To turn too swiftly
will make us drift
into a sea of hate.
Let us carefully balance
like the antique pin
on which the angels danced;
let us not feel vengeance.

"Domine Jesu Christe"
"Lord Jesus Christ"

XI. FERTORIUM: HOSTIAS (Second Friend)

For a time, we must turn to stone:
to stone, Mother;
Sister, turn to stone;
Friend, to stone.
Turn to stone, heart,
that once felt gladness in his presence.
Be a stone, hand,
that clasped his shoulder in respect.
Be a stone, eyes,
that enjoyed the runner's body
swiftly moving.
Ears, be stones,
that felt more than heard
the drumming of the feet.
Be a stone, sleep,
that brings the nightmare back
to us.
Turn, turn all of us to stone.
Let us be.

"Hostias et preces tibi"

*"Sacrifice and prayer
unto you"*

XII. SANCTUS (First Friend)

He was one of us; yet he was not.   *"Sanctus, sanctus, sanctus"*
By custom alone we coaxed from   *"Holy, holy, holy"*
    harsh indifferent
ground the seed and no one cared whether
we lived or died and all the while the flies
got fatter on the people's blood; yet he
understood before us all what was
to be done to put an end to grief.
He was blessed, and so are we.

XIII. AGNUS DEI (The Nun)

With effort I remember him.   *"Agnus Dei, qui tollis*
Carefully, I trace his features,   *peccata mundi"*
see the runner's open look and smile,
hear his quiet tones.   *"Lamb of God, that takest*
I see his truncated body   *away the sins of the world"*
and tenderly seal his dismembered feet
upon his legs and see him whole again.
I scrutinize his palms:
the marks are there.
I kiss them.
I watch his walk, see his stride,
see his feet break into a run.
I see him whole again.
I desire his being whole again.
I see myself. I watch myself
with a lover's eye. I desire myself
whole again. I tell myself
I am whole and alive. I wash
myself in aliveness. I wash myself
in being. Vengeance
falls from me: strategic
anger takes its place.

XIV. LUX AETERNA (The Mother)

Soon a new dream will come
from the men and women
crushed by the dying State,
nails driven into hands and feet,
or roaming on a soil they do not own.
The struggle does not stop.
It moves me on.
It ebbs and flows in the dark
blood of the world.
It pushes me up on the high tide
of its pain.
It engulfs us but cannot destroy us.

(First Friend)
The legacy remains unstained.

(Second Friend)
The legacy remains a fact.

"Lux aeterna luceat eis"

*"Light eternal shine down
upon them"*

XV. LIBERA ME (All)

In our palms, on the balls
of each one of our feet,
a pulse beats heavily.
In our ankle bones,
a soreness comes and goes.
But we move on, our souls intact.

"Libera me de morte aeterna"
"Deliver me from eternal death"

IV. Voices in the Blood

Voices in the Blood

(A Dramatic Narrative)

I. THE NARRATOR

The routines of life. A warm bath and the flower of the skin
opening. Thick butter on black bread. Hot words and a cuff
on the head. Spying on deer stepping quietly out of the
woods of a purple evening and as quietly stepping back. Wild
blackberries picked in late summer floating in cream, eaten
with a friend under the porch. An alphabet as familiar as
touches and smells of brothers and sisters. Books worn with
fingerprints and marks of sweat.

II. THE CZECH GRANDMOTHER

Suddenly none of that —
an early morning roundup
by Nazi guards
into the waiting trains
blinds drawn
mothers crying out
outside, even we older ones
throwing ourselves
on the tracks, curses,
bodies bumping
across the ties,
and by midday, our mourning
souls stained
like our smocks,
the last child on board —
my little sapling —
and the train
moving off
until it shrinks
into the pupil of the eye
and the children become a smudge
against the sky
and the whistle
a mouthless cry.

III. THE NARRATOR

This is the meaning:
Children were selected —
    those with specified proportions
    cast of nose
    coloring
    strength
    the proper quotient —
and carried with contempt
to the center of corrupt empire,
to clinics called "homes,"
where, their mother tongues torn out,
their names and customs erased,
they became the seed of the Superrace.

IV. THE POLISH MOTHER

Like mushrooms deep
inside the forest,
succulent, medicinal,
with no one there
to gather them in —
we women at a stroke
were left without the purposes
that had unfolded from
our flesh, and found
that life goes on.

One night
the forest burned
behind Bielsk;
next day
they took the children.
We ran after, calling,
crying, trying to touch
but the SS turned on us
like winter wolves

and the bared fang
of bayonets held us at bay.
Our own, taken away.
No matter how fierce,
before this evil
we were rabbits.
We cried out louder,
threw ourselves on the tracks,
were beaten and dragged off.
First the men, now children.

In dreams I still see
her legs and mine close
beneath the blue quilt
watching deer
of a summer night
glide from our woods
across the lawn
to sip at the barn trough.
We loved that time
together, she and I.

In secret each of us
has done unconfessed acts.
I myself have rampaged
through the woods
to join the night
in a fantastic mass
that brings her from the dead.

After thirty years
life should close
upon a wound.
Time should heal.
Out of the far field
last year, long barren ground,
a small spring
suddenly burst
scattering
wild flowers all around.

V. THE ONCE-POLISH DAUGHTER

Consider a small
bird fresh from
twigs and burrs

of a woodland nest,
trilling through violets
and jack-in-the-pulpits,

stalking insects over
moss-covered roots,
all of a sudden

tossed by a gale out
over the sea, driven
back and forth

with no halt to
the flapping of wings,
no sense of known

textures and smells,
its eyes popping,
oiled by panic;

and should it spot
the mast of a derelict,
it must alight.

So torn from home
that day, and forever,
our masters stern

and forbidding, we
became children of
the Third Reich —

and the wrenched past
died in us. New
language, customs,

dress, new names.
Those who remained
airborne disappeared.

I was adopted.
This is my home:
my husband, two sons.

That Polish woman
who claims me
for her daughter

her eyes anguished
probably like
the eyes of martyrs

staring upward
in icons —
I cannot help her.

VI. THE NARRATOR

O Czechoslovakia! O Poland!
your children torn
like pages from the family Bible,
like little sparrows lost
over oceans, their wide eyes
bobbing on the waves —
there is no measure for this
corruption at the core
so immense that neither
justice, vengeance, nor prayer
can settle the score.

VII. ERNIE, THE SUDETEN GERMAN GARDENER

Roots inching outward
have by early spring
trapped the sweet earth
in their meanderings.
Stems surging upward
burst into air
and leaves and buds
suddenly appear.

She was in that spring
when a child's eyes open wide
to the truth of things,
and her Self — so newly found —
she could not give up.
Her natural pride
became intransigence:
she had to die.

They tied her feet and hands —
their reprimand
to a child who refused
her German lesson.
Czech is my language,
Ernie, she said.
You understand me.
I'll never learn their ways!

And always after punishment
she'd run to where
the greenhouse used to be
to help me with my chores.
She talked about her home,
the Grandma who canned
blackberries in a white smock
stained with polka dots.

Finally they tied her up
in the tool shed. I brought
her the blue blanket
left by the Polish girl.
The dogs shot her next day
during language hour.
She is buried there
beneath the yellow flowers.

VIII. THE NARRATOR

Two thousand children stolen from Poland,
        more from Czechoslovakia,
        those "not fit" — shot
    Jewish children and their teachers
        sang songs
        marching into ovens —
            in my dreams
                their ashes whisper the words
                    of my terror
                                forever
    and the rest of them   slaves
        hammered in posts and barbed wire
        the grey planks with knotholes
            where the wind cried
            out of the Nazi night
    like iced birds   they huddled
        beneath thin blankets
            and in the morning
                            the dying
                            buried the dead.

IX. THE YOUNG MAN

Nights
in the camp
were cold.

Each morning
those assigned
would pry

our comrades' bodies
apart
and dump them

in a mass grave
dug daily
in the field;

and after the dirt
had been thrown
back into the ditch,

I recall,
as the morning sun
shone down on those

fresh filled fields,
bodies that were
partly frozen

thawed
and the field of dirt
would start to ripple,

then move in waves,
then in a single
spasm of pain

until death
began and earth
grew still again.

X. THE CZECH GRANDMOTHER

I neither fear nor greet death
now, have even lulled
the pain, held its hand
for thirty years. At first,
war over, I huddled,
a frightened deer, close
to home, ears tensed
to catch the hunter's step.
Laid out our village dead,
properly. Boarded up
the burnt-out rooms.
Planted and harvested.
Mournèd. No men.
No children at our feet.
Just women like me
past childbearing.

Guns silent, the camps opened.
Remnants of youth appeared.
Later a few babies were born.
Like flowers out of the rubble.
I went to town to learn
midwifery just for them,
hoping they would keep
coming, hoping to deliver
them; wash that sweet
skin; swaddle them in
my blue shawl; help
pale young breasts
feed, and from cornered eyes
coax smiles: build
other ways than death.

I love them as my own —
as I loved her whose mouth
I darkened with berry juice.
They call me Granny.
That helps me survive.
What better work to do than turn
dead ground into garden?
The eye of evil stares
hard but I outstared it
with birth and re-birth.
My death, in peace,
will make it shut for now.

V. Carpentry

Carpentry

I.

At an advanced age,
over the hill for the union
wage, my carpenter friend
apprenticed herself
to herself, and learned
the trade.

I have watched her
adroitly
eyeing
tongue and groove sidings
or with her fingers tracing
miniature turrets
like byzantine prayers rising
from the cherrywood mantel
or measuring the small drawers
with white ceramic knobs —
all artifacts hallowing
nature because crafted
by hands for beauty.

II.

My apprenticeship began
as a child: I would
drift through home
on a Saturday afternoon,
alone, conversing with the
spirit of the lintel,
or sit in the paneled seat
in the upstairs window
and tap out a code,

or wheel three times
a semi-circle back
and forth on the palm-sized
newal post and marvel
at the finished feel of oak.

III.

Later I studied trees
and found them compatible

As the tall autumn maples,
branches strong for climbing,
camouflaged in rust brown leaves,

and in the wintertime stripped
of all ornament, a black
lattice where juncos perched
above the snow cover.

As the bright burst
of blonde forsythia
in the gush of green spring
that melted my frozen eyes;

or the pink parasols
of the dogwood blooms twirling
trapped in abrupt
gusts of wet wind
that set me twirling.

In Big Bear once
I watched the grave forbearance
of the dark pine tops
looming, serious intimates,
from the chasm beside
the fog-soaked road.

IV.

In the garden
not long ago
on my hands and knees
preparing the soil
for the yellow flowers
I dug with my hands
next to a pepper root
and unearthed a tunnel
the length and width
of my arm,
and buried in that womb
up to my elbow
and lying down against
the soft earth,
I waited for the graft
to take place.
It did.

V.

Leaves burst forth;
leaves die, drop,
become earth.
The tree secures life:
deep in the ground
roots crash down
through stone;
the trunk thickens,
branches stoke the air.
The secrets
are still there
learned one by one
by discontinuous generations,
and that primordial print
that comes to us in magic
now moves to majesty:
primitive mind
grows a center eye
that sees itself seeing,
knows itself knowing
yet seeing, knowing,
and feeling itself,
still converses with trees.
This seems a proper trade:
a natural apprenticeship.

VI.

The sharp tool
in the hand of
each carpenter
fashions form,
several,
from the vast
trunk of nature.
 Forms of the Self
are the Self,
indivisible,
sprouting forth,
dropping down
dying
reborn.
The hand trembles
in the doing —
the thing fashioned
so fragile
so costly
so barely
alive.

The Green Ceramic Frog

FOR S. K.

The green ceramic frog,
        your last year's gift,
stares across the room
        that ripples out
a deep and shadowy pond
        from where it squats
on the lily pad
        on the window seat
beneath the Chinese fern —
        its eyes glassy and green.

Below the surface
        of the quiet pool
lives the queen
        of cheerful solitude,
fated to roam
        between a friendly commerce
with the creatures on the shore
        and a lurking alone
with the purple shapes
        of her own murky place.
Rich pins of moonlight
        catch up her greying hair;
her tinsel flesh
        scarcely touches air.

Words like red lilies
        float above her
and longings for changes
        dart like goldfish
back and forth
        between the chambers of her heart:
to be a perfect song
        strummed by Segovia;

a wooden spoon
        that dishes up potato soup;
to be a dolmen
        brooding on the plain;

or like an icon,
        its own sun when suns burn out;
or a rocky path that nicks
        steep peaks with stubborn grace;
a fog that rising drifts
        away from its grey starting place.

The green eyes see
        still more:
the bumping of shore
        and air and water creatures,
their rubbings and growlings,
        their grumblings and nuzzlings;
that is, rituals
        of love and anger;
note laughter
        that jars birds from branches;
watch the pleasureable doings
        of the daily task,
the unabashed delight
        in the common ways of things.

And even before each change
        is accomplished fact,
the eyes have recorded
        the invisible fact
of the source
        of the longing for change:
the need for the perpetual leaving
        of ritual, body, and thing;

and the perpetual return
        from such a meandering.
Of the perpetual leaving
        as, say,
a song, a spoon, a dolmen,
        an icon, a path, a fog;
and the perpetual coming back —
        pool under one arm
and in her pack
        the green ceramic frog.

Song of the Cockroach

Cr—cr—cr—cr—
your scissornails
are not quick enough
to pinch our sturdy bodies;
your sprays not strong enough
to stop our lightening raids.

Remember —
we have survived the shifting
mountains, the desert storms, the ice;
have watched wars
and the indolence of children.
Know who think us magic, who not.

In the shadow
of the new built sphinx
we moved from the dung pile
at the camel trough
to the cutting board
near the open fire

where fatty pieces of meat
sweet-roasted
in their juices
lie
neatly
side by side.

From there a simple step
of centuries finds us
crawling up inside the walls
of your own home, past studs
and plaster board, through
cracks into the pantry.

Inside the darkness of your
cupboard — a kind of Egypt
of the senses — spiced with
string bags of onions,
garlic buds and celery flakes,
we take note of ancient herbs.

Over long spaghetti rods we frolic.
In the cornmeal and flour,
our young appear;
between the paper plates and cups
and the breakfast cereals
and cocoa, we pass on our observations.

Understand — we wait until you
close your daylight out
and then in surreptitious
multitudes, serene in our
eternity, creep out
to rot the staples of your lives.

Cinderella's Sister

South of Vienna the train swerves around
mountainous curves that rouse the traveler

from her morning doze. Out the window I
can see vast skies and peaks. From here the end

cars look like a toy train on a toy track
climbing a plaster mountain side. I am

comparing customs with Frau Schneider, her
legs crossed, one hand on her hip, the other

.smoking. Suddenly leaning her ample
body forward, both feet planted firmly

on the floor, an elbow propped on each knee,
breasts squashed between like crumpled roses, she

tells me how it is with love; how it flares
up like a rare disease and then dies down

in the haze of daily life; how affairs
will come but the household must still run on

time — affairs of the heart must never get
out of hand (the children, after all, must

be bathed and put to bed); how the first is
the most exciting — sensual meetings

in darkened bistros, learning to disguise
love bites on the neck, then hurrying home

to supervise cook's soup; titillation
the day you meet his wife at the garden

party, and, of course, she does not suspect;
even the crises with your husband

will all be survived. After all, you will
be a veteran survivor of his

affairs. No question of separation;
you made a family with this person.

Her dark eyes sparkle from the fragments of
her life — the people and the things managed,

and skillfully. This is the way it is,
and she is prepared and in full control.

At midday she spreads a white cloth between
us and on it places dark bread, pickles,

salami, beer, a sharp knife, and two blue
napkins. I accept her invitation.

Hundreds of feet below, the green valley
sprawls out and random peaks rise from the floor.

Occasionally a miniature
stone castle perches atop such a spire

with moat and keep, turret and drawbridge, and
crenelated tower. I imagine

an aging Cinderella with her prince
moving through the huge hallways hung with rugs,

or sitting in the family room edged in
green wreaths on gold leaf walls, a marble

fireplace, a writing desk, satin pillows
scattered on the floor; and them before the

fire, she embroidering, wondering how
to sneak away to the garden house that

night; he smoking, savoring his conquest
of the chamber maid as she made the bed

that morning; and in the hallway four boys
roughhousing, six through fifteen, the girl now

married, and expecting her first one soon;
and in the courtyard outside, the formal

garden waits to bloom on cue. Beyond the
grey walls, flowers and grasses roll full tilt

on top of each other down the meadow
slopes, their roots grappling in the moist dark earth.

The stones sweat beneath the fire, and the grooved
drawbridge rattles over the murk below.

All is in its proper place — the play is
underway; the next thirty years are set.

The train lurches around another curve
and slightly nauseous from the sudden spin

I focus on a flaw in the window
glass and see my reflection there, my eyes

attentive; beyond, the landscape speeds by:
gone stone castle, moat, turret, and tower;

gone hallways hung with rugs, green wreaths, marble
fireplace, desk, satin pillows on the floor.

Across from me Frau Schneider lightly snores,
her crossed legs flapping gently with the train.

I look down at my big brown hands resting
in my lap, my swimmer's legs etched beneath

the soft blue folds of my dress, my big red
walking shoes planted firmly on the floor.

I breathe deep, relax. The nausea leaves.
I look forward to my destination.

VI. Sonatina:
Andante Cantabile

Sonatina:
Andante Cantabile

1.

You appear out of the muzzle of a gun,
How To Make A Revolution in your hand;
across the Commons table, inquire what
I read. We settle in to talk about it.
Outside the leaves turn brown; grackles alight
on iced branches; when spring comes, wrens.

 Meantime out of the dining hall they drag
chic Jacques back to France in a straitjacket;
and Mark, ten years in classics, doles out gold
from the family mine: each week the taxi waits
to take his laundry. And Etienne, ex-priest,
blue eyes pools, the hairs on his hand tremble;
he studies to be a sensualist. Momentarily, Biffie
will stride by, a volley ball in her hands.

2.

I used to hunt for God in obscure ways:
church, Bach cantatas, and the like
but when we met I tracked my senses down
in parks, pressed between you and wrought-iron fences,
or in the Village, in the alley near Barrow, dancing
on damp walls between squatting garbage
cans and staring cats; or in the imbroglio
of our bodies moving gear-like on the bed.

From these moving parts sweat
flows but no god comes —
only you
shoulders hunched
mouth open
eyes fiercely blank.

3.

Far from your love that turned me renegade
I came to Siena, fortress of bells and walls,
a blast to God from the plain, a town on rock,

of thin streets and stones, worn down
by centuries of tears and penitent feet,
but a city that has tasted graced fruit:

here Catherine coaxed lilies, whispered roses
from the dirt, heard leaf and limb in hymns,
and Columbini's flame flashed in letters:

"Dear Friend, How can I express the affection
and charity my heart and soul feel towards you,
transforming everything through devotion.
May it enter your soul like flame, with gentle penetration."

Oh, it is with reverence that I return the gift of myself.

4. "LE BAL À BOUGIVAL"

Ah, there she is twirling her pink skirts,
her orange bonnet fluttering on her tilted face,
and there he is holding her around her back,
jaw intense, eyes hidden by the straw hat.

But couldn't we pretend in the quickening
of the green light through the leaves
in front of the excited faces of the drinkers,
couldn't we pretend that their love
growing with the rhythm of the dance
moved out beyond that sociable cafe,

unseen at first because convention wills
some reference to a waltz, out beyond that
music to join the light, the soaring breeze
that moves beyond the shelter of the trees?

5.

Orphaned, you swaddled our newborn in blankets
remembering your own, and the worn carved cradle
hung from the ceiling; the fierce tartar eyes
peering at you, delighted; the Hush! Hush!;

Even the beads of milk from the quilted breast,
the lullabys and low chuckles; later before
he could be stopped, grandfather's jesting curse,
and grandmother, turning the icon to the wall.

These were good things to be told and repeated
as best one can once ripped apart by war,
alien custom, and the dry eyes of time.

This is the breast you guided into our child's
mouth. This poem celebrates your delight in nursing
and your wish to be father, and mother.

6.

What storms they have to weather still in this
the perfect city nestled in palms and sun
but stillborn under anglo eyes, each beach
the shoreline for destroyers. I traveled west
with eastern eyes, a heritage in books,
a temperament formed by the passions of weather,
the death of leaves and the stark branch: it
sheathed in ice, it snow-covered, a sounding
board for the twitter of juncos; in torrential spring
troups of tulips and violets; and down in the woods
jack-in-the-pulpits peeking up through moss.

What more is your loss? A memory of skies?
Of wheat and rye? The great river watering the steppes?
The dance of your people, their freedom baked in daily
                              bread?

7.

You whose body was a message from the war
reading saber wound, gun butt on the neck;
who brought a spirit clean of underbrush,
a path burned bare to the farthest target;

who stepping down from the train of sorrow
sang songs of love, and of the wolf's path
apart in the purple gulch of snow (no matter
war turned those gulches red, and songs ceased);

who chose to cross another range with no
horizon but your now familiar death —

we have grasped these things together: this child,
these books, this bed — dear common things, of grace.

The imprint of your hand shapes a world
past sorrow: I touch you when I hold a flower.

8.

It was in your eyes, Love, I first believed:
bright and steady and black, a lover's eye;
and later the benediction hummed from the loft
summoning spirit through rose window prisms.

Is there a hand that greets the birds? a fist
against the whip? an eye on the flight of wrens?
feet racing fish? These exist there.

And later, as general lover, the eye light,
two diamond gears rotating towards me —
me hunched over in fear — made a clear
demand towards Everything — Essence.

Once in an empty room staring back
from the glass a halo of sparks lunged out
at me from those luminous and unfamiliar eyes.

9.

Some wounds never heal you said and I felt
a rush of love for you in that life before
we met, a youth at war, out of the orphanage
of pain. The train chugged south. Onions
dotted the field, onions and blood and dead horse
and crammed in boxcars the others huddled,
eyes hovering over thin faces,
and the fear there — and in the field row
upon row of onions. The bitterness growing.
You gathered them up as if they were apples and you
quartered them like grandma used to quarter
pippins and you passed them out to the hungry. Now
I cannot eat onions you said. Thirty years
is not time enough to heal some wounds.

10.

Dear, come, let us loaf on Vashon,
that island where timber bristles high
into the sky, and boat and tide
drift into the curlew's cry.

We will lie side by side on the beach,
hear the sea sift sighs through the trees,
see the sun burst seed, winds cast it free;
let grains of sand slide between our toes,

stars slip through half-closed eyes;
plot, sing songs, dream up new states
where grown-ups play, and flags fly poetry.

O victorious weeks — where the crest
of the waves froth into beaded continents
that float for a wink and then break up.

11.

Inevitable. The path lost in thorns.
The witch in wait. Crumbs eaten.
We need more than a star: things must be
signposts — the black chair you sat in,

the sculpture of lovers . . . If everything
changes, we plummet a comet orbiting earth,
crisscrossing forever alien space
desperate to touch on familiar turf.

Then Self senses the drift of Self
and Terror looms in the liquefaction of form.
Will you be my friend forever? I asked
twenty years ago. Forever is not over.

Yet things must be signposts,
must be certain, at least some.

12.

And so we have come to twenty years of love —
beyond song, dark eyes, love-making in murphy
beds, against fence posts, behind the stern
stone lions in the city library park;

having run a course between the dull gulp
of domesticity and the ceaseless terminations
of this neurotic time; no his/her snapshot,
he taller, she, an orchid on the memory of a bosom.

Having come through so far — what is love?

In the summer garden two butterflies careen
wings touching gently over the dying flower.
Above its nest the eagle hovers, sights
another like itself, crags away wheeling,
and diving warns it of some foe.

13.

Outside the pepper trails silver green;
raucous lantana flaunt yellow-red bouquets;
a fly careens over the lone carnation
all innocence in its white fragrance.

We can see them from this study jammed
with our own nature: sprouting books, jars
of clips and bands, pipes on the horseshoe
plaque, an orange calendar marked June.

Papers lie scattered on the desk like leaves
from the tree in the picture of St. Francis
his young hands stretched out to birds. Here
are fragments of work, an alphabet of mind.

When the wind is high, a branch of the pepper taps
on the pane, signals a reminder of our place.

14.

There is a note inside my book
on Tolstoy with a quote which tells
of a helmeted marble head, boldly chiseled,
a slight smile on curved lips, that crumbles
to dust beneath the viewer's stern gaze.
The gift-giver, struck with this omen
for the dissolution of "ossified bonds" and
"marble straitjackets," has inscribed the book
with love to me in whom he saw both friend
and lover. Years later, I remember the gift
as a rare sign of the right to outstare
time and the works of men. So this was the lover's
intent! And if this can be between two,
it seems the peg to hang revolutions on.